A Magic Ride in Foozbah-Land ©1995 by Jean Betschart

All rights reserved. Except for brief passages for review purposes, no part of this publication may be reproduced, stored in a retrieval system, or transmitted, in any form or by any means, electronic, photocopying, recording, or otherwise, without the prior written permission of CHRONIMED Publishing.

Betschart, Jean
A Magic Ride in Foozbah-Land: An Inside Look at Diabetes./ Jean Betschart, M.N., R.N., C.O.E.

ISBN: 978-0-471-34755-2

Edited by: Donna Hoel
Creative Direction: Robert W. Schmitt
Illustration: Jackie Urbanovic
Production Manager: Claire Lewis
Printed in the United States of America

Published by
CHRONIMED Publishing, Inc.
P.O. Box 59032
Minneapolis, MN 55459-9686

Julie and Jeff just wanted to play. To be in the hospital on such a nice day was no fun. But still they needed to know a lot about health before they could go.

Nurse Kelly smiled
at the kids and sighed.
"I've tried and tried
and I've tried and tried . . . ."
And they looked up
with such hopeful faces;
They had listened and studied
and sat in their places.

Her job was to teach them
and hope they would learn.
She'd been nice, she'd been sweet,
she'd been tough, she'd been stern.
But they had to cover
so very much . . .
Blood testing and shots
and food groups and such.

Not candy, not sodas,
not skipping their Wheaties
Had caused them to get
this disease, diabetes.
It had to be dealt with;
they had to be taught
to do blood tests,
learn food groups,
and even a shot.

"I know what I need!
Here's what we'll do!
To the Magic-Machine!"
she said to the two.
They looked at each other
with a note of surprise.
Was she mad? Was she smart?
Was she nuts? Was she wise?

They followed her closely,
both holding her hand,
To a door that said:
"This way to Fantasy-Land."
"We're going on a trip.
We'll have a great time.
You'll learn quite a lot
in this capsule of mine."

"Don't be scared," Kelly said.
"Don't ever fear.
For, my dears, I'll go with you.
Oh yes, I am here!
We'll all just jump in,
and off we will go
On a wonderful ride.
(Yes, your parents will know.)"

"Oh! What an adventure!
Soon you will see,
Things that go on
inside you and me!
Now that you're tucked
all safe inside,
We're ready to go
on our magic ride."

"Just flip this switch, and watch us all shrink very, very, very small."
"Who'll flip the switch?" Jeff asked. "I will . . . ." And soon they looked just like a pill!

With tea and peas
and mashed potatoes,
Lettuce, beef,
and red tomatoes,
The magic capsule flew along.
Kelly yelled, "Wheeee!!"
and hummed a song.

They landed
with a plop in goo.
"Where are we now?
What shall we do?"
"We're in his stomach
and we'll soon be churning.
(He ate so much,
it's probably burning.)"

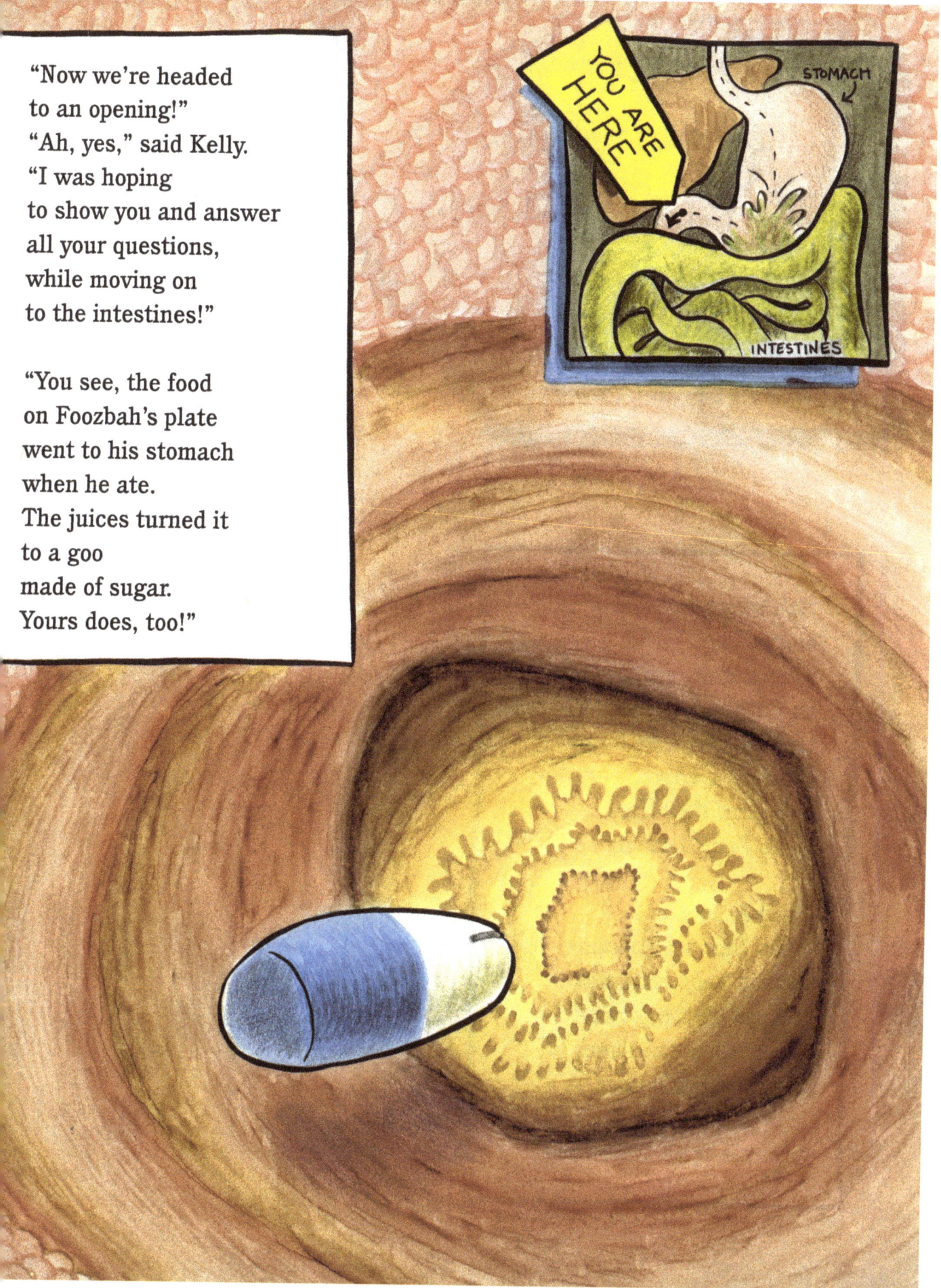

"It's rough and lumpy,
bumpy here."
The capsule caught
on a mound, where
they watched the sugar
swirl all around
and go in the lumps
(with quite a sound).

Then Kelly said,
"Now here's a question.
What's happening now
in Foozbah's digestion?
We'll follow the sugar
to see where it goes.
Into the blood,
from his brain to his toes."

UR LEFT
ATELETS
T WORK
HONK! HONK!
WHAT'S GOING ON? SUNDAY DRIVER!
LEMME THROUGH!
ARGH!
CARBON DIOXIDE TRANSFER
SUGAR EXPRESS
ACK!
GOING OUR WAY?
OUTTA MY WAY, FATS!
SUGAR EXPRESS

"What's all this stuff? What does it do?"
"Well," said Kelly, "It makes you YOU! This funny shape is called a cell. Cells work together to keep you well."

"Now, see the sugar. There's a bunch! (Cause Foozbah ate a great big lunch.) The cells you see are hungry. They need that sugar for energy!"

"I still don't get it!" Julie cried. "How does that sugar get inside?" She asked again, "How's it get in?" And Kelly said, "With in-su-lin."

"It's really not
too hard to do,"
Jeff said.
"I've already had a few.
Sometimes I feel
a little poke.
But it hardly hurts—
and that's no joke."

"Now pay attention
here inside,
while I slow down
our exciting ride.
I want a moment
to tell you two
new things you're going
to have to do."

YOU ARE...
OUT THERE
SOMEWHERE!

"What else?" asked Julie
as they flew,
looking around
at everything new.
The capsule kept going,
moving quite fast.
And Jeff shouted,
"Wow! This is a blast!"

"You'll have to watch
the foods you eat.
Right foods, right times,
not many sweets.
And test your blood
at times with care
so we can tell
how much sugar's there.

"You'll also have
to test your pee,
because we are going
to have to see
if ketones are there.
It's important to do
each morning
and if you have the flu."

"Ketones are
a nasty stuff.
They build up fast,
make you throw up.
But most of the time
they won't be there.
And if they're not,
you don't have to care.

"OK, kids!
We have to hustle.
I want to show you
Foozbah's muscle.
Muscle cells are
busy working.
Not one of those little guys
is shirking."

"Insulin hooks
right on to the cell,
and opens it up.
It works very well.
The sugar travels
right inside.
The cells can eat,"
Kelly said, with pride.

"Foozbah's walking,
catching a ball,
touching his toes,
and stretching and all.
Muscle cells need sugar
to do their task.
Insulin helps them
get it fast!"

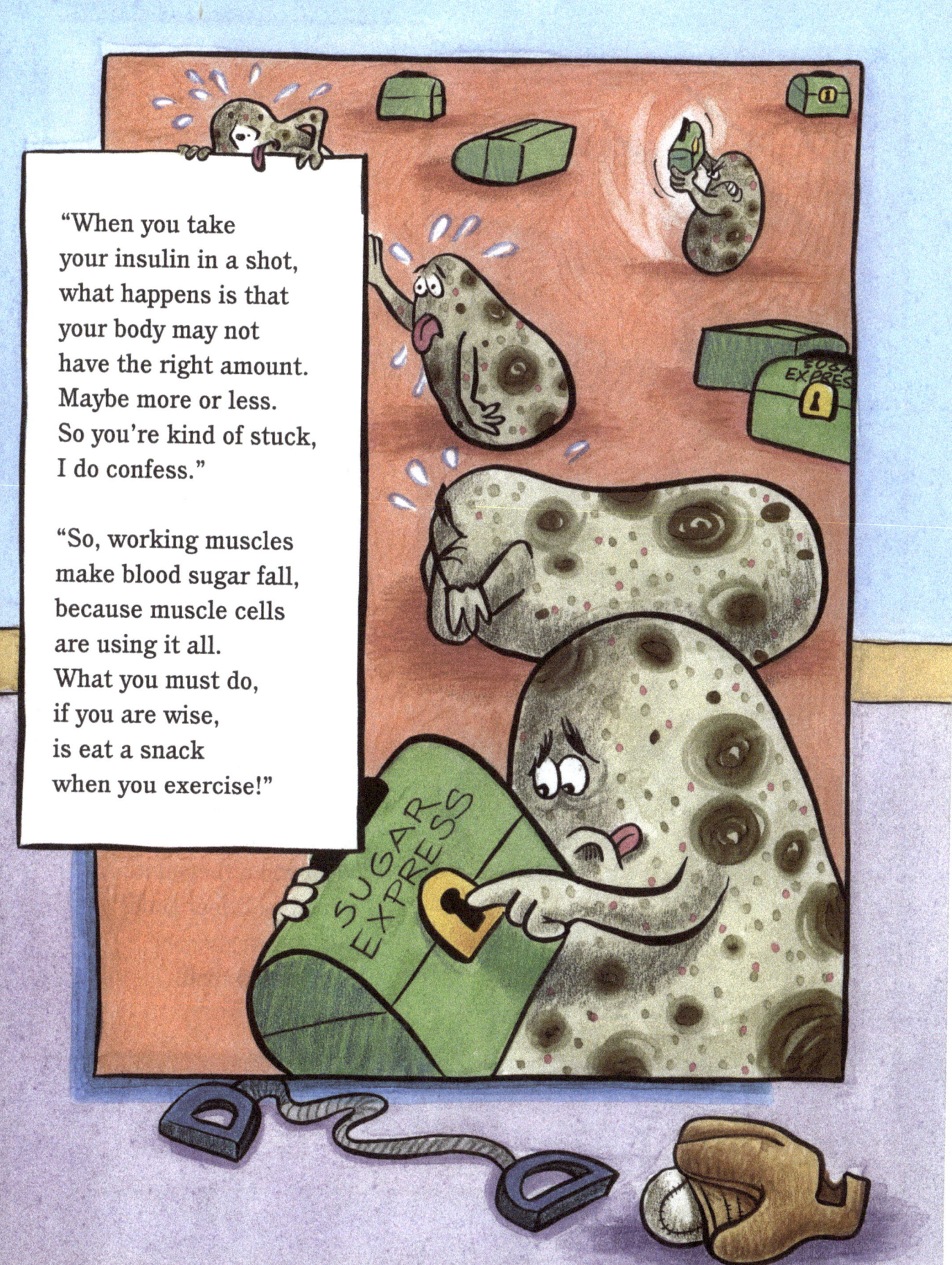

"When you take your insulin in a shot, what happens is that your body may not have the right amount. Maybe more or less. So you're kind of stuck, I do confess."

"So, working muscles make blood sugar fall, because muscle cells are using it all. What you must do, if you are wise, is eat a snack when you exercise!"

"Enough of that now,
we'll learn more tomorrow.
Our trip now must end,"
she said with sorrow.
"Do I make sense?
Do you understand?
Are you learning at all
in Foozbah-Land?"

"Yes! Now I think
we understand
the reason for
our meal plan.
Our food and drinks,
both cold and hot,
must match the insulin
in our shot."

"Great!" said Kelly,
with a shout.
(At times things
really do work out!)
"And when they match,
you should feel good!"
She was so pleased
they understood!

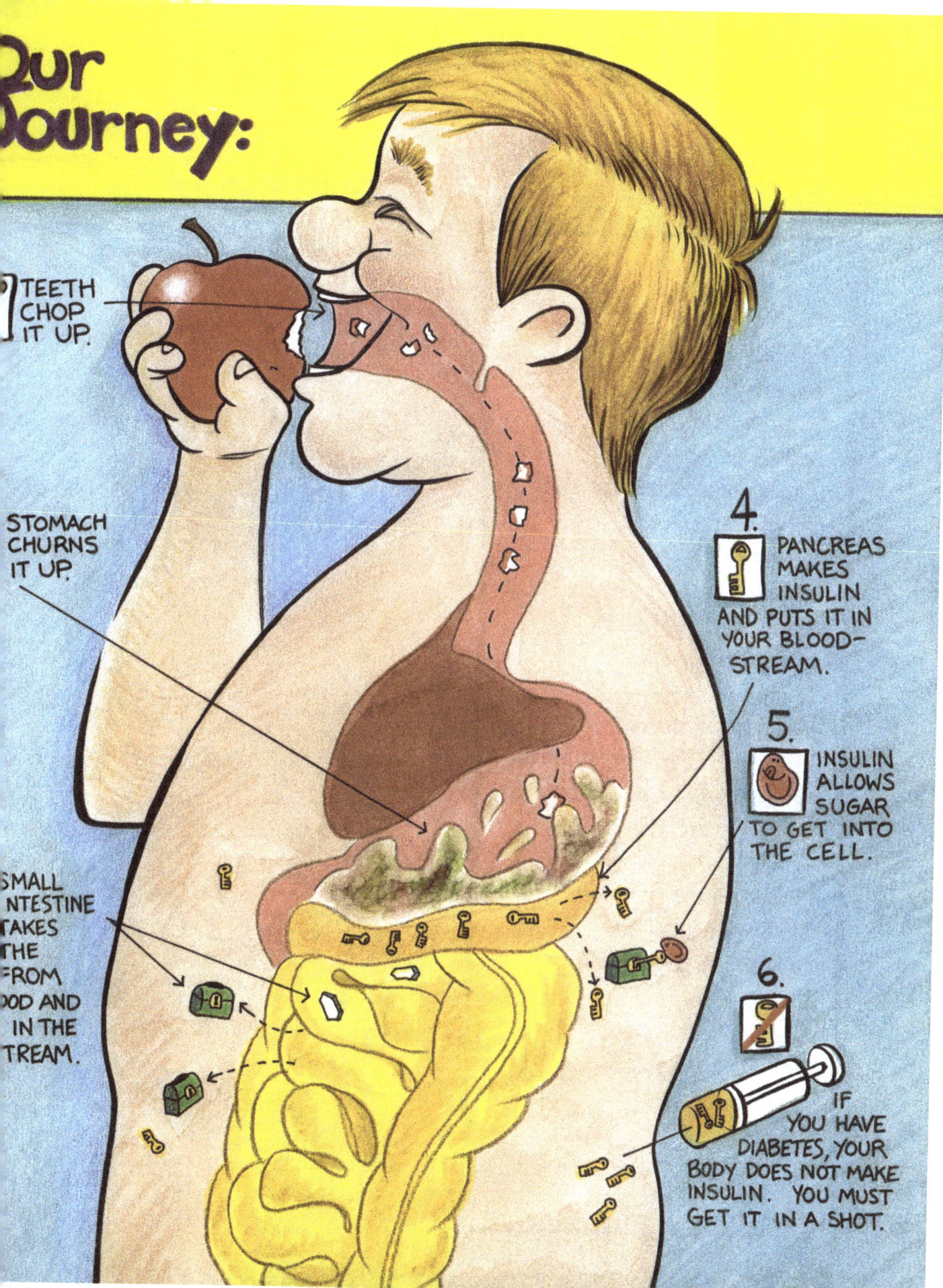

"Well, kids,
this has been a blast!
You knew, though,
that it wouldn't last.
Before we leave,
is there something you two
would really, really
like to do?"

"Of course," Jeff said,
with a little wink.
"I want to see
just how we think!"
Julie said, "I've always wanted
to know what exactly happens
when I grow!"

"I might have guessed,"
Nurse Kelly sighed.
"Those are different
magic rides.
We must come back
and go those ways
on some other
magic days."

"Let's flip the switch.
And here we go!
Feel like we're going
a little slow?"
They were back in
the classroom now
they learned,
surprised how fast
they had returned.

They blinked
and then looked all around.
For a second,
no one made a sound.
"Could the magic ride
have really been?"
Jeff thought. "But now
I know about insulin."

They thought about food and how it turns to sugar, and then remembered they learned that it goes to the blood to feed each cell. And that insulin helps to keep you well.

"I understand now about shots and why I'm going to have to always try to eat right and test and exercise too, so I can be healthy my whole life through."

Nurse Kelly smiled.
She knew they knew.
And that their
understanding grew.
"That's all for today.
It's time to go.
Good job, nice work.
You're great, you know!"

"Your parents will be
so very pleased
to hear what you've learned
(and how!)" she teased.
"Of course, I doubt
if they'll believe
the story I'm sure
you two will weave."

www.ingramcontent.com/pod-product-compliance
Lightning Source LLC
Chambersburg PA
CBHW081502040426
42446CB00016B/3363